Evidence for the Existence of God

Benjamin Chang

Second Edition

© 2014 Benjamin Chang

First Published 2014
Second Edition 2015

Cover design by Michelle Kwong ©

All rights reserved.

No part of this publication may be reproduced, stored in a retrieval system, or transmitted in any way or by any means, including photocopying or recording without the written permission of the copyright holder.

ISBN: 978-1-326-90047-2

Printed by Lulu Press, Inc.

With thanks to

Prof. Kin-Chow Chang

Joanna Higginson

Michelle Kwong

David Lake

Hannah Mead

And special thanks to Isabelle Keane
whose idea it was for me to write this book

This book is dedicated to anyone who has never looked into the evidence for the existence of God before, and would like a place to start.

For more articles by Benjamin Chang, visit:
www.benjaminchangblog.com

Contents

Preface to the 2nd Edition ... 5

Introduction ... 6

1. Scientific Evidence Part 1
   The Existence of the Universe: The Cosmological Argument ... 8

2. Scientific Evidence Part 2
   The Fine-Tuning of the Universe: The Teleological Argument ... 18

3. Philosophical Evidence
   The Morality of Humanity: The Moral Argument ... 25

4. Historical Evidence Part 1
   The Historical Jesus: The Lewis Trilemma ... 33

5. Historical Evidence Part 2
   The Resurrection: The Minimal Facts Argument ... 41

Conclusion ... 53

Recommended Reading ... 54

Notes ... 56

Preface to the 2nd Edition

When I first published *Evidence for the Existence of God* almost exactly one year ago, I could have never expected the attention it was going to draw. Since the 1st edition, I have had the privilege of speaking to a number of audiences on the matters covered in this book, and have had many great conversations and debates with friends, colleagues and total strangers about the evidence I present.

I owe a great deal of gratitude to the many Christians, agnostics, atheists, Muslims and those of other beliefs who took the time to read *Evidence for the Existence of God* or attend one of my talks and afterwards, discussed and debated the arguments with me. Over the past year, it has felt like every detail of every argument has been scrutinised, analysed and debated with fervent rigor.

In this 2nd edition, I have added a couple more objections (plus rebuttals) to the Cosmological Argument in chapter 1 that have come up in reply to the 1st edition. I have also tweaked some parts of the other chapters in response to objections and criticisms that have arisen in dialogue with critics.

C. S. Lewis once said *"Christianity, if false, is of no importance, and if true, of infinite importance. The only thing it cannot be is moderately important."* If the existence of God is not worth continuing to debate, I have no idea what is!

Introduction

From a young age, I never liked being told what to do- by anyone, but particularly by my parents. Whether it came to homework, socialising, sports or tidying my room, my default setting was always to do the opposite of what they told me. Unsurprisingly, this mentality crept into my view of religion. I grew up in a Christian home, and I have been going to church since before I can remember. However, from a young age, I began to doubt the stories my parents had taught me and my Sunday school teachers had made us sing about and re-enact in silly homemade costumes. In some regards, I became an atheist as a child. I was rarely condemning or mocking of religious people. However, as a wannabe scientist, I found it difficult to understand how anyone could believe in anything, without hard evidence. God seemed to be the epitome of this- an invisible, inaudible, unmeasurable, indescribable God seemed to be totally empirically unverifiable. Therefore believing in Him, without evidence, or even the hope of evidence, was decidedly a stretch too far for me.

However, as you can probably deduce from the title of this booklet, things changed. In my late teens, I began to have the urge to look into the evidence for and against the existence of God. I started digging into recorded debates, lectures, literature and the like, aiming to look objectively at whether there was indeed evidence for Christianity, atheism, or some other worldview. What I discovered totally transformed my life. After around six months of intense research I came to a crazy conclusion: the evidence pointed to Christianity! I found that the scientific, philosophical and historical evidence all converged on Christianity as the most evidence-based worldview there is. In fact, in the face of all this evidence, I gradually realised that it would have taken more blind faith to hold onto my atheism, than to convert to Christianity.

This little booklet is a brief walk through the most convincing pieces of evidence I came across when I was searching for the truth. We will take a rapid helicopter ride through the disciplines of Science, Philosophy and History, and look at what each one has to say about the possible existence of God. *Evidence for the Existence of God* was always meant to be a short overview of the arguments for God's existence, and libraries of books have been written on the chapter titles alone. However, I hope that these fifty pages or so will act as an introduction to some of the evidence for God, and maybe even whet your appetite to look deeper into the arguments.

So here begins the evidence that totally changed my life.

1. Scientific Evidence Part 1

The Existence of the Universe:
The Cosmological Argument

This argument (sometimes called the *Kalam Cosmological Argument)* is an ancient one that can be traced in some form, all the way back to Plato and Aristotle[1]. However, it still remains a hugely popular and, in my view, very powerful piece of evidence in favour of the existence of God. And the evidence cannot be more accessible; it is the simply the existence of the universe.

The argument is based on two premises:

- Premise 1: Everything that has a beginning has a cause
- Premise 2: The universe had a beginning

Premise 1: Everything that has a beginning has a cause

This premise is fairly uncontroversial and intuitive. Our experience informs us that if an object, state or process begins, it always begins for a reason. In fact, this assumption is the foundation of most experimental science, which looks to deduce the causes of observations.

We can also assess this premise by looking at its negation (or alternative). If the negation of a statement is false, it logically follows that the statement must be true. And of course, if the negation of a statement is true, the statement itself must be false.

The negation of Premise 1 would be "*not* everything that has a beginning has a cause", or in other words "something can come from nothing". However this is certainly not a logical thing to say. Nothing cannot *create* anything, because nothing cannot *do* anything. To suggest that something can come from nothing is, to put it bluntly, worse than magic. At least when a magician pulls a rabbit out of a hat, we have the magician to posit as the cause (never mind the hat!).[2]

Therefore, on philosophical, scientific and experiential grounds, most critics conclude that Premise 1 is true: everything that has a beginning has a cause.

Premise 2: The universe had a beginning

Although my field is Human Biology, I find the physics of the start of the universe absolutely fascinating. Over recent years, a huge amount of evidence has come to the fore clearly indicating that the universe had a beginning, roughly 13.7 billion years ago. I shall briefly touch on some of this evidence, which has come from three very different scientific fields: cosmological physics, molecular chemistry and applied mathematics.

18th Century cosmology revolutionised the ancient debate of whether the universe had a beginning or not, with the discovery of the Doppler shift. This was the finding that the wavelengths of electromagnetic radiation coming from distant galaxies and stars indicated that the universe is in a state of cosmic expansion. When extrapolated into the past, this resulted in the theory that the universe started with a single "explosion" from an infinitesimally small point. We of course now commonly call this the "Big Bang Theory". The Big Bang Theory totally transformed cosmology, by switching the mainstream scientific view that the universe was eternal, to that of the universe having a beginning.

Evidence for a beginning of the universe also comes from a fundamental principle of chemistry: the 2nd Law of Thermodynamics. The 2nd Law states that the magnitude of the entropy (a measure of "disorder") of the universe is increasing. However, this Law requires there to have been a beginning to the universe a finite time ago, for if the universe has existed from eternity past, the universe would be totally disordered by now. This would produce a universe devoid of any fluctuations of enthalpy (measure of "heat energy"), which is certainly not what we observe today. As Prof. Stephen Hawking remarked:

"it [the 2nd Law of Thermodynamics] indicates that there must have been a beginning. Otherwise, the universe would be in a state of complete disorder by now, and everything would be at the same temperature."[3]

In 2003, another weighty piece of evidence emerged from the field of applied mathematics. Leading scientists Arvind Borde, Alan Guth and Alexander Vilenkin mathematically *proved* that any universe that is in an average state of cosmic expansion cannot be infinite in the past, but must have had a beginning[4]. Vilenkin's conclusion was blunt:

"It is said that an argument is what convinces reasonable men and a proof is what it takes to convince even an unreasonable man. With the proof now in place, cosmologists can no longer hide behind the possibility of a past-eternal universe. There is no escape: they have to face the problem of a cosmic beginning."[5]

The volume and breadth of scientific evidence mean that scientists virtually unanimously agree that the universe had a beginning.

Conclusion

Once we have established that the two premises are true, we can then add a conclusion.

- Premise 1: Everything that has a beginning has a cause
- Premise 2: The universe had a beginning
- Conclusion: Therefore the universe had a cause

The universe having a cause may not seem like a significant statement given the premises, and it certainly does not prove God's existence on its own. However, we can now look at what a cause of the universe would have been like. From what we know about the universe, we can deduce several characteristics of its cause[6]:

- The universe encompasses the entire "material world". Therefore the cause of the universe must be *immaterial*.
- The universe includes within it all of the spatial dimensions. Therefore the cause of the universe has to be unbound by the spatial dimensions, so must be *dimensionless* or *infinite*.
- The universe also includes within it, all of the temporal dimensions. (Einstein's theory of Special Relativity showed that space and time are actually two components of the same substance, unimaginatively called "spacetime".) Therefore a cause of the universe has to be unbound by the temporal dimensions, so must be *timeless*, or *eternal*.
- Finally the cause of the universe must be immensely *powerful*, to have created all that we see around us in the universe.

So science leads us to look for a cause of the universe that is immaterial, dimensionless, infinite, eternal and incomprehensibly powerful. One does not need to be a theist to realise that this sounds like a comprehensive description of God!

Commonest Objections to the Cosmological Argument

#1 Who created God?

This is the most common objection or criticism to the Cosmological Argument in my experience. However, it seems to be very peculiar. Premise 1 does not say "everything has a cause"; rather it states "everything *that has a beginning* has a cause". In the Christian worldview (and indeed in the majority of other theistic worldviews) God is eternal- He has always existed. Therefore as an eternal being, He does not need a cause because He has simply existed from eternity past. This principle does not just apply to God. For the vast majority of human history, mainstream science has believed that the universe has always existed. Because of this, scientists did not need to hypothesise a cause of the universe- its eternality meant they did not have to.

So if God is eternal, He does not come under the category "everything that has a beginning" and therefore does not need a cause.

#2 Could the cause of the universe be the multiverse?

The Multiverse Hypothesis is something that we will revisit in a little more detail in the next chapter. However, there are some points worth mentioning with respect to the Cosmological Argument.

The Multiverse Hypothesis states that there exists many universes in a kind of "universe ensemble", of which our universe is a part. These universes may be being generated by some sort of "random universe generator", which creates different universes with different properties.

There is very little, if any, empirical evidence from any field that indicates the existence of the multiverse. This has led some theistic apologists to accuse subscribers to the hypothesis of having "blind faith".

However, an interesting result spawned from the Borde-Guth-Vilenkin theorem[4] which mathematically proved that the universe had a beginning. The theorem implies that even if our universe is one of many in a multiverse, the multiverse must also have had an absolute beginning and could not be past eternal. Therefore, postulating a multiverse does not get rid of the need for a cause; it simply puts the beginning further back in time.

#3 Could the universe have created itself?

This is the view held by Prof. Stephen Hawking, who, in his controversial book *The Grand Design* (in which he also declares that *"philosophy is dead"*) writes: *"Because there is a law such as gravity, the universe can and will create itself out of nothing"*[7]

Putting aside the point that the law of gravity is clearly not "nothing", Hawking's view also contains a significant logical fallacy, which Prof. John Lennox wittily points out:

"the statement "the universe can and will create itself from nothing" is self-contradictory. If I say, "X creates Y," this presupposes the existence of X in the first place in order to bring Y into existence. If I say "X creates X," I presuppose the existence of X in order to account for the existence of X. To presuppose the existence of the universe to account for its existence is logically incoherent. What this shows is that nonsense remains nonsense even when talked by world-famous scientists. It also shows that a little bit of philosophy might have helped."[8]

The idea that the universe created itself is simply logically incoherent.

#4 Could the laws of the universe have changed at some point in history, leading to the appearance of a beginning?

This is a fascinating conjecture, but one which throws up some uncomfortable issues for those who study physics.

The Big Bang Theory is what some call a theory of "the Science of History". Other Science of History theories include biological evolution, radioactive carbon dating, etc. Science of History subjects are all based on one fundamental assumption: we can look into the past by looking at the physical processes of the present and extrapolating backwards. However, this requires the laws of the universe to have remained constant throughout the existence of the universe. If the laws of the universe changed at some point in history, our extrapolations could only be valid from after the point of change; i.e. we would not be able to deduce anything from before the change. So the idea that the laws of the universe could change is an awkward one, because it would throw into question the very foundations of the Big Bang Theory, as well as everything else we know about the past universe.

However, there is a more serious issue with this hypothesis. If the universe did change from some unknown state into the classical spacetime that we observe, we would have to conclude that the universe was in a state of quantum instability before the change. However, an unstable universe at the quantum level could not have existed from eternity past[9]. As physicists Anthony Aguirre and John Kehayias summarised in their 2013 paper:

"it is very difficult to devise a system – especially a quantum one – that does nothing "forever," then evolves. A truly stationary or periodic quantum state, which would last forever, would never evolve, whereas one with any instability will not endure for an indefinite time."[10]

Speculating a universal state change does not negate the need for a cause of the universe. It (like the multiverse hypothesis) simply puts the start date further back in time.

#5 Why would the law of cause and effect apply to something outside the universe, and therefore outside the laws of physics?

Objections #5 and #6 are interesting metaphysical objections to Premise 1: "Everything that has a beginning has a cause". These require a little bit of in-depth unpacking, so feel free to skip over these two sections if metaphysics does not interest you.

Some opponents to the Cosmological Argument argue that Premise 1 is true of everything *in* the universe, but not *of* the universe[11]. This is because it is generally believed that the laws of physics only apply within the boundaries of the universe.

However, proponents of this view fail to understand the rationale behind Premise 1. I would argue that Premise 1 is true, not because it is *empirically* verifiable, but because it is *logically* verifiable. In other words, the evidence for Premise 1 comes not from experimentation and testable observations, but from logical necessity which stands independent of the laws of physics. An analogous example could be the statement: "There are no married bachelors in existence". We know this statement is true, not because of testable evidence from repeatable experiments, but because it has to be true on logical grounds. This statement would thus still be true, even outside the universe where (we believe) the laws of physics do not apply. Or to put it another way: there cannot be any married bachelors, even outside the universe.

Similarly, I would argue that Premise 1 is true on logical grounds (i.e. something cannot ever come from nothing), not empirical grounds. Therefore it would still apply to events outside the universe and not bound by the laws of physics, such as the creation of the universe itself.

#6 Why would the law of cause and effect apply to something that is not bound by time (such as the time dimension itself)?

This is a paraphrase of an argument popularised by philosopher Prof. Adolf Grünbaum in 1990[12]. Grünbaum argued that the law of cause and effect requires a pre-existing time dimension, because a cause must always *precede* its effect in time. Therefore, the postulation of a cause of the universe (containing the time dimension) is nonsensical, because this would require causation occurring independent of the existence of time.

However, many philosophers contest the premise that "a cause must always precede its effect". This was famously illustrated by Immanuel Kant who described a heavy metal ball resting on a fluffed cushion[13]. The ball resting on the cushion *caused* an indentation in the cushion. However, the ball resting did not *precede* the indentation. Rather, this is a good example of *simultaneous* or *atemporal* causation (i.e. a cause and its effect happening at the same time).

We find a similar situation with the creation of the universe. I would argue that God's creation of the universe happened simultaneously with the universe coming into existence. Therefore, the cause and the effect happened simultaneously, so there is no need for a pre-existing time dimension at the beginning of the universe.

#7 Surely the Cosmological Argument does not lead to Christianity alone. It could lead to the belief in the God of Islam, Mormonism and many others.

I totally agree with this point. The Cosmological Argument indicates God's existence. However, it does not say enough about God's character for us to find out if the true God is that of Christianity, Islam or some other religion. In order to deduce if one of these religions has an accurate depiction of God, we need to look at other evidence about

God's character (rather than simply for His existence). We will be coming to this in chapters 3-5.

2. Scientific Evidence Part 2

The Fine-Tuning of the Universe:
The Teleological Argument

The Teleological Argument is potentially even older than the Cosmological Argument, with many believing that it arose with Plato's teacher, Socrates. The argument can be simply summarised in four words: *the universe appears designed.*

Physics has discovered that the universe is governed by a plethora of universal physical constants and quantities (e.g. the speed of light, the gravitational constant, Planck's constant, etc.). These are numbers that (we presume) hold constant throughout the universe and allow scientists to write equations. On analysis, we find that these constants all fall within a literally incomprehensibly narrow range of life-permitting values. I shall provide two brief examples, but of course the list is very long.

The *weak nuclear force* is one of the four fundamental forces of nature, and is responsible for radioactive decay of subatomic particles. The *weak nuclear force* is so finely-tuned that an alteration in its value by 1 part in 10^{100} would prevent the formation of stable atoms. This would obviously lead to a universe that does not permit the existence of life.

Another universal constant is the *cosmological constant* which drives the acceleration of the expansion of the universe. An alteration of the *cosmological constant* by 1 part in 10^{120} would cause the universe to expand either too quickly or slowly. Both would prevent star formation and the universe would be rendered life-prohibiting.

As the philosopher Dr. William Lane Craig summarises:

"The range of life-permitting values for the constants and quantities [of the universe] is extremely narrow. If the value of even one of these constants or quantities were to be altered by a hair's breadth, the delicate balance required for the existence of life would be upset and the universe would be life-prohibiting."[1]

Imagine, by some bizarre and worrying turn of events, I am playing a game involving a lottery machine and a handgun. The lottery machine contains 99 identical black balls and 1 white ball and after jumbling the balls, one is selected at random. If the white ball is selected, nothing happens; however, if a black ball is selected, I get shot. Imagine the ball is drawn and to my surprise and relief, the white ball is chosen. After mopping my brow (and probably changing my underwear), it would undoubtedly dawn on me that the lottery machine had possibly been rigged for my survival. I would not be certain, but the improbability of my survival would definitely raise my suspicions of cheating (not that I would launch a complaint on this occasion).

Imagine now, that the game described above is actually 1 round of 100, and each time the process is repeated with 99 black balls and 1 white ball. 100 times the lottery machine is jumbled, and 100 times the white ball is "randomly" selected. After the 10th time the white ball is selected, I would be pretty certain that the machine was rigged for my survival, and after the 50th round, I think I would probably start to get quite comfortable with the game.

This is the situation we find ourselves in when we analyse the physical constants of the universe. Each constant seems finely-tuned for our survival, and the probability of every constant being fine-tuned for permissibility of life is so astronomically small that it seems logical to deduce that the universe has been rigged for our survival. However, in order for the universe to be rigged, it requires a rigger who wants us to survive. A universe rigger who desires our survival sounds very much like God[2].

Before we turn to some common objections to the Teleological Argument there is a point that needs to be made regarding objections.

Imagine that a man and his son are walking down a sandy beach at dusk. There is no-one in sight and all that they can hear is the sound of the waves. They turn a corner made by a little out-pouching of the cliff-face, and they see, written in the sand, the word "sternocleidomastoid". If you are a biologist, you will probably know what this word means[3]. However, they, like most people, do not recognise the word. The father and son look at the writing, and start to ponder to each other. *What does it mean? Who wrote it? Why did they write it? How did they write it?*

However, one thing is unquestionable in the pair's minds: somebody wrote it. Perhaps someone could argue that it is possible (albeit astronomically improbable) that the word came to be there by the random deposition of sand by the waves that so happened to create a word that means something to a small group of people. This may be *possible* as an explanation of the word in the sand, but would one really describe it as *logical*?

Many objections that I have heard to the Teleological Argument stem from the notion that "improbability" does not mean "impossibility". However, such advocates often find that they are kicking against their own logical minds, in order to avoid what is, in my view, the most logical explanation to the fine-tuning of the universe: a cosmic fine-tuner.

Commonest Objections to the Teleological Argument

#1 Doesn't the Anthropic Principle give a reasonable explanation to the fine-tuning of the universe?

The Anthropic Principle was developed with respect to the fine-tuning of the universe, by the cosmologists John Barrow and Frank Tipler in 1986. They summarised their position as the following:

"Our existence imposes a stringent selection effect upon the type of Universe we could ever expect to observe and document. Many observations of the natural world, although remarkable a priori, can be seen in this light as inevitable consequences of our own existence"[4].

In other words, we have to expect that the universe has life-permitting properties, because we are alive to observe them.

However, this argument is somewhat attacking a straw man. Let us go back to the lottery machine analogy. Imagine the lottery machine contains 100 balls, but instead of coloured, they are now each numbered from 1 to 100. I then take 100 volunteers and allocate them a number between 1 and 100, and tell them: "I will select one ball at random, and if the ball selected corresponds to your number, you will win a prize" (a far more enjoyable game!). So we proceed; I jumble the balls and randomly select the ball with number 37, and the person who has been allocated the number 37 wins the prize. It would be bizarre for the person who won to then hypothesise that the machine was rigged for their winning. The probability of number 37 being selected was very small, but the probability of *someone* winning was 100%. This is the equivalent of postulating the Anthropic Principle; if all possible universes are equally probable, then it is safe to assume that at least one will come out as life-permitting. We have been "drawn" the life-permitting universe, so we do not need to postulate a rigger- just chance.

However the Teleological Argument is not looking at the probability of our universe getting the life-permitting properties, over another universe getting them, like the person winning the prize over someone else. Rather, the argument looks at the probability of getting a life-permitting universe, over a life-prohibiting universe, like selecting the white lottery ball in the 99 black balls, repeatedly 100 times. Because we are talking about the (very) unequal probabilities of getting a life-permitting and life-prohibiting universe, the Anthropic Principle simply does not apply to this argument.

However, a more serious issue with the Anthropic Principle is that it relies on the Multiverse Hypothesis with an extra characteristic: a random universe generator. In order for the Anthropic Principle to be relevant to the start of the universe, we must presuppose some sort of mechanism that produces an infinite number of universes that all have different constants, in order for our universe to "come up". However, a universe generator of this sort would still have to fulfil all the criteria of the cause of our universe mentioned in chapter 1. It must be immaterial, dimensionless, infinite, eternal and incomprehensibly powerful. This still seems to be a detailed description of God.

#2 Who designed the designer?

The atheist biologist Prof. Richard Dawkins describes this question as "the central argument" of his famous, religion-slamming book *The God Delusion*. He helpfully goes on to summarise the argument in a series of six bullet points[5]:

1. *One of the greatest challenges to the human intellect has been to explain how the complex, improbable appearance of design in the universe arises.*
2. *The natural temptation is to attribute the appearance of design to actual design itself.*

3. The temptation is a false one because the designer hypothesis immediately raises the larger problem of **who designed the designer**.
4. The most ingenious and powerful explanation is Darwinian evolution by natural selection.
5. We don't have an equivalent explanation for physics.
6. We should not give up the hope of a better explanation arising in physics, something as powerful as Darwinism is for biology.

Therefore, God almost certainly does not exist.

As many people have pointed out, the conclusion *"Therefore, God almost certainly does not exist"* comes out of nowhere, and I have no idea how the conclusion follows the six premises.

However, more to the point *"who designed the designer"* is one of the most bizarre arguments a scientist can make. The reason is simple; in order to accept an explanation of an observation as the best, you do not need an explanation of the explanation. This is one of the most basic principles of the philosophy of science.

Let us go back to the beach writing analogy. I think everyone would agree that the best explanation of the word "sternocleidomastoid" written in the sand is that a human being wrote it. However, we do not need to have an explanation of who wrote, why they wrote, how they wrote it, or indeed what the word means, in order to accept the explanation that someone wrote it. By Dawkins' logic, "someone wrote it" cannot be the best explanation of the writing the sand, because we do not have an explanation (as to the origin of the writer) of the explanation (that someone wrote in the sand).

In fact, this argument leads immediately to an infinite regress of explanations, and the total obliteration of science. Because before we can accept an explanation of any observation, we would first need an explanation of the explanation. But before we can accept the explanation of the explanation, we would first need an explanation of the explanation of the explanation. But before we can accept the explanation of the explanation of the explanation, we would first need an explanation of the explanation of the explanation of the explanation. And before we can accept… (you get the idea)[6].

In putting forward this argument, Dawkins needs to presuppose a principle that leads to the immediate demolition of the science that he and I base our careers on.

To accept a fine-tuner as an explanation of the fine-tuning of the universe seems to me to be a far more logical (and scientific!) position than to reject it by Dawkins' reasoning.

3. Philosophical Evidence

The Morality of Humanity:
The Moral Argument

As a medical student, moral values and duties are matters continually on my mind and in my lectures. However, the development of naturalism as a widespread worldview has led to some uncomfortable and challenging ideas about morality.

The Moral Argument is based on two premises:

- Premise 1: If the moral code exists, a transcendent, authoritative moral code-giver exists
- Premise 2: The moral code exists

Premise 1: If the moral code exists, a transcendent, authoritative moral code-giver exists

Atheism usually comes with the worldview of naturalism, which is the belief that everything in the universe is physical (so there is no spiritual realm, for example). If an atheist believed in a spiritual realm, most people would not call them an "atheist". Throughout history, naturalists have come to a realisation that with naturalism comes the death of morality. Friedrich Nietzsche, the atheist philosopher who proclaimed the death of God, is often quoted to have said *"Morality is just a fiction used by the herd of inferior human beings to hold back the few superior men"*, while Prof. Richard Dawkins eloquently writes in his 1995 book *River out of Eden*:

"In a universe of blind physical forces and genetic replication, some people are going to get hurt, and other people are going to get lucky; and you won't find any rhyme or reason to it, nor any justice. The universe we observe has precisely the properties we should expect if there is at bottom... no evil and no good. Nothing but blind pitiless indifference. DNA neither knows nor cares. DNA just is, and we dance to its music."[1]

In a sense, I agree whole-heartedly with Nietzsche and Dawkins. In the naturalistic worldview, morality cannot exist. If our entire human being is exclusively physical, then we are nothing more than biological machines enacting what we are programmed, by our DNA, to do. The act of one person murdering another is as morally neutral as an avalanche killing a skier; the avalanche and the murderer are simply doing what they are programmed to do by their internal physical mechanisms.

So where does the moral code come from? The Scottish enlightenment philosopher David Hume famously pointed out that the scientific laws and the moral laws are on two different and unbridgeable levels of existence[2]. He argued that the scientific laws describe what *is* and *is not*, while the moral laws describe what *ought* and *ought not* to be. As C. S. Lewis explained:

*"The [scientific] laws of nature... only mean "what Nature, in fact, does." But if you turn to the [Moral] Law of Human Nature, it is a different matter. That law certainly does not mean "what human beings, in fact, do"; for many of them do not obey this law at all, and none of them obey it completely. The law of gravity tells you what stones do if you drop them; but the Law of Human Nature tells you what human beings ought to do and do not. In other words, when you are dealing with humans, **something else comes in above and beyond the actual***

facts. *You have the facts (how men do behave) and you also have something else (how they ought to behave)."*[3]

In order to make the leap from what *is* to what *ought* to be, one needs to posit a "moral code giver" that transcends human behaviour, and has the authority to impart the moral code to humans[4]. However, a transcendent moral code giver who has the authority to give us the moral code is, in essence, a theistic God.

Premise 2: The moral code exists

As we look at the world around us, it becomes quickly apparent that a huge number of our institutions, structures, organisations and programmes are foundationally based on the existence of the moral code. In the UK, we have a massive and publically treasured National Health Service. However, any health service anywhere in the world, whether tax-payer, private, or charity funded, is based on a foundational moral value: human health is a good thing. And this single moral value continues to be the reason why some of the most intellectual people in society dedicate their lives to administering healthcare as doctors and nurses.

We can also look to the other enormous institution of our age- the judiciary system. Whether national, international, criminal or civil, all laws are based on a fundamental moral principle: justice is a good thing. Like healthcare, this single moral value continues to lead the brightest minds to careers in which enforcing justice is the ultimate goal.

These are just two of many huge human institutions which are entirely based upon the assumption that the moral code exists. Health and justice cannot be good things if there is no such thing as "good".

We also can look at our own personal experience to find that the moral code is an integral part of our human existence. It seems logical that the repulsion and grief we feel when we witness or hear about acts of torture, torment or terrorism are grounded in violations of a moral code intrinsic to humanity. Similarly, when we applaud or feel moved by significant acts of heroism, humanity or humility, it is because a real moral good has been fulfilled.

Therefore, from the sociological and psychological evidence, I believe that it is far more probable than not that the moral code exists.

The Moral Argument can thus be concluded with:

- Premise 1: If the moral code exists, a transcendent, authoritative moral code-giver exists
- Premise 2: The moral code exists
- Conclusion: Therefore, a transcendent, authoritative moral code-giver exists

Commonest Objections to the Moral Argument

#1 Hasn't morality been evolved?

The Theory of Evolution and its theological implications are huge topics which I do not have the space to look at in much detail in this little booklet[5]. In short, the Theory of Macroevolution states that we all are descendants of a common unicellular ancestor, and biodiversity is a result of genetic mutation and selection of characteristics that allow individual organisms to survive to the point of reproduction. This theory can be used to explain why some snakes produce venom (to prevent their predation) or why some rodents hibernate (so they do not have to look for food when there isn't any). However, the moral code cannot be explained as a product of evolution alone for one simple reason- it often does not work in the individual's self-interest. Evolution selects characteristics that enhance the chance of the individual's survival to reproduction. However the moral code seems often to work *against* self-preservation. For example, if I were walking past a lake and saw a desperate person who had fallen in and was splashing around shouting for help, my moral instinct would compel me to help them. And if it came to it, I might jump in to try to rescue them, at the expense of my own self-preservation. This kind of altruistic behaviour cannot be explained by evolution alone, which only functions for the preservation of oneself and one's genes.

#2 Could the moral code be the result of social nurture?

In my experience, this is the mainstream view of non-theistic morality: it is simply a product of our social conditioning. However, this view seems to involve a redefining of what most people know as morality.

There are many examples of codes produced by social norms and structures; we called these "social codes". For example, it is a social code that men should not go into the women's toilets. This social code exists because if I (as a man) were to break the code, there would be social consequences for me and those around me. However, a social code also means that if one can avoid the social consequences, the social code does not apply. So if I were a night watchman at a museum and all the other night watchmen were male, then once the museum had been closed and locked for the night, there would be nothing wrong with me using the women's toilets. The social consequences are absent, so the social code does not apply.

However, a "moral code" is different. A moral code states that certain things are right or wrong *regardless* of the social consequences. So the moral code would state that it is immoral for me to kill a homeless person with no friends, no family and no job, even if there were no social consequences. In other words, the moral code *transcends* social structures.

We can look back to the judiciary system to see a striking example of the transcendence of the moral code. Although a lot of laws are confined to nation states, we also have international laws and human rights. It follows that the moral code: "justice is a good thing", transcends social structures. In fact, history is filled with people who have suffered and died for the moral duty of justice in societies they were not brought up in (so not "conditioned" by).

Our personal experience also shows us that some codes transcend social structures. When I go abroad, there are some codes that I have to adapt to (for example, if I was in Singapore, I would not be seen eating in an underground train). However, there are some codes that would always remain the same in my mind, regardless of the society I ended up in. For example, I would always submit to the moral code that murder is wrong, regardless of which society I found myself in.

Therefore, from structures such as the judiciary system, as well as personal experience, we can deduce that some codes transcend social structures. However, if we have a transcendent code, we require a transcendent code-giver.

#3 How can the moral code be transcendent, when people have different ideas of what is moral and immoral?

#4 Is it not true to say that people get their morals, at least in part, from other people e.g. parents?

These two arguments are quite different, but both make the same mistake of confusing *epistemology* with *ontology*.

Epistemology is the study of the creation and dissemination of knowledge and beliefs[6], while ontology is the study of being and existence[6]. Let's say (for the sake of argument) that the moral code exists ontologically. Different people may then discover parts of the moral code in different ways and times. People may also feel that they have discovered some of the moral code, but really have gotten it wrong, and some people may never gain awareness of the moral code at all. However, none of these possible epistemological (belief) scenarios would impact the ontological (actual) existence of the moral code. So "different people have different morals" and "people get their morals from different people/places" (statements of epistemology) would not nullify the evidence for the actual existence of the moral code.

Incidentally, the Christian worldview clearly states that God reveals His moral code to us in different ways, including teaching from other people[7], reading the Bible[8] (which Christians believe to be the word of God), and also having an in-built awareness that some things are morally right and wrong[9].

#5 Why should I submit to God's moral code? How would I know that God's code is superior to a code written by me or someone else?

These are fantastic questions that cut to the heart of the Christian worldview. In order for us to know if God's moral code is worth submitting to, we need to find out two things:

1. Does God know best?
2. Does God mean best?

Both need to be true in order for God's moral code to be worth submitting to. If God knows best but does not mean best, he is evil. If God means best but does not know best, he is incompetent. And an evil or incompetent god is not one I would want to obey!

1. Does God know best?

Simply from the first two arguments in this booklet, I think the answer would be yes. We have already deduced that God is eternal, infinite, incomprehensibly powerful, creator of the universe (and therefore also of you and I), capable of rigging the constants of the universe, and desires our survival. Without opening the Bible, I think one can reasonably conclude that God is powerful and knowledgeable enough to know what is best for us. The Bible goes a little bit further and says that

God is all-seeing[10] and all-knowing[11]. However, this is an idea of God that is pretty unanimously accepted; if God exists He is probably all-seeing and all-knowing by definition. So the notion that "God knows best" is fairly uncontroversial.

2. Does God mean best?

This is a much more contested notion; does God really have our best interests at heart? This is the fundamental difference between *deism* and *theism*. Deism is the belief in a god who creates and then "leaves us to it" and has no intention of involving himself with creation. Theism is the belief in a God who cares for and "gets involved" with His creation.

Christianity makes a huge claim in answer to the question "Does God mean best?" Romans 5:8 says: *"God demonstrates his own love for us in this: while we were still sinners, Christ died for us"*[12]

The Christian claim is that, c.2000 years ago, God took human form in the man of Jesus who then died for us[13]. Out of all the gestures of love I have come across in my life, I think the biggest is the willingness of one person to die for another. This is how the Bible says God proved that He means best for us.

Obviously this raises many questions. *Did Jesus really exist? Was He really God in human form? Did He really die for us?*

We are going to investigate all of these questions (and more) in the final two chapters of this booklet. If these huge claims turn out to be true, then we have firm grounds to believe that God both knows best and means best, and therefore his moral code is worth our submission.

4. Historical Evidence Part 1

The Historical Jesus:
The Lewis Trilemma

The first three arguments in this book (the Cosmological, Teleological and Moral Arguments) were ones I came across when I first researched into Christianity to ascertain if it had any legs to stand on. Although I found them quite convincing, they did not compel me to conversion to Christianity. However, these last two arguments (the Lewis Trilemma and Minimal Facts Argument) did. The historical man of Jesus, who lived c.2000 years ago, is the central claim of Christianity and one which can be analysed with rigor.

Did Jesus ever exist?

It is the view of some people (though the number is small) that Jesus never existed. However, among scholars, the fact of Jesus' existence is virtually incontrovertible. Even the most militant of atheist historians almost unanimously accept that Jesus existed.

The Emperor of Rome during Jesus' ministerial life was Caesar Tiberius. Tiberius' name is mentioned in 10 different trusted historical documents that date to the Ancient Era. In comparison, there are 40 different documents that mention Jesus' name[1].

In *The God Delusion*, Prof. Richard Dawkins wrote *"It is even possible to mount a serious...historical case that Jesus never lived at all"*[2]. However, such was the extent of his subsequent hammering by the historical profession that during his second recorded debate with Prof. John Lennox, Dawkins uttered the staggering words *"Maybe I alluded to the possibility that some historians think Jesus never existed. I take that back! Jesus existed."*[3]

Did Jesus claim to be God?

The Christian doctrine of the incarnation states that c.2000 years ago, God took human form in the man of Jesus. Therefore, it is logical to first investigate whether Jesus made this claim about Himself.

As one would expect, the Bible contains several accounts of Jesus claiming explicitly and implicitly to be God. In John 10:30 Jesus says *"I and the Father are one"*[4] ("The Father" was one of Jesus' names for God), while in John 8:58, after being asked *"who do you think you are?"* Jesus replied *"Very truly I tell you, before Abraham was born, I am!"*[5] This statement appears to be grammatically incorrect; "I am" seems it ought to be "I was" or "I have been". "I am" is most likely a reference to God's Old Testament name for Himself "Yahweh" which literally means "I am". The Jews to whom Jesus was speaking knew this to be the case, for they immediately tried to stone him for blasphemy[5].

It is also clear from study of extra-biblical accounts that 1st Century Christians genuinely believed that Jesus was God. There are many recorded creeds (established repeated sayings) from the early church that explicitly reference the divinity of Jesus. On studying these creeds, the historical scholar, Prof. Gary Habermas concludes:

"These creeds reveal that the church did not simply teach Jesus' deity a generation later, as is so often repeated in contemporary theology, because this doctrine is definitely present in the earliest church...The

best explanation for these creeds is that they properly represent Jesus' own teachings."[6]

We also have trusted recorded accounts from enemies of the church that corroborate the Christian accounts of Jesus' claims to be God. For example Pliny the Younger, who was governor of Bithynia (northwest Turkey) and an important Roman historian, wrote:

*"I interrogated them [Christians] whether they were in fact Christians; if they confessed it, I repeated the question twice, adding the threat of capital punishment; if they still persevered, I ordered them to be executed... they sang in alternate verses a hymn to Christ, **as to a god".***[7]

Lucian of Samosata was a 2nd Century Greek satirist who wrote:

*"The Christians, you know, **worship** a man to this day - the distinguished personage who introduced their novel rites, and was crucified on that account...[they] **deny the gods of Greece**, and **worship the crucified sage**, and live after his laws."*[8]

Given the notion that God could take human form was so alien to the traditional Jewish teaching, it is logical to deduce that the Christian belief that Jesus was God spawned from Jesus' explicit and unambiguous claims to be the creator God of the universe.

Wasn't Jesus just a great moral teacher?

In my experience, this is the commonest-held belief about Jesus- that he was a great human moral teacher, but nothing more. However, given the evidence that Jesus claimed to be God, this stance is seriously undermined. Someone who was just a human but claimed to be God would not be someone from whom I would want to take moral guidance! C. S. Lewis summarised the position with characteristic eloquence:

> *"I am trying here to prevent anyone saying the really foolish thing that people often say about Him: "I'm ready to accept Jesus as a great moral teacher, but I don't accept His claim to be God." That is the one thing we must not say. A man who said the sort of things Jesus said would not be a great moral teacher. He would either be a lunatic — on a level with the man who says he is a poached egg — or else he would be the Devil of Hell. You must make your choice. Either this man was, and is, the Son of God: or else a madman or something worse. You can shut Him up for a fool, you can spit at Him and kill Him as a demon; or you can fall at His feet and call Him Lord and God. But let us not come with any patronizing nonsense about His being a great human teacher. He has not left that open to us. He did not intend to"*[9]

Another commonly held belief is that Jesus was a prophet or messenger from God. This is the view held by most Muslims in accordance with their holy book, the Qur'an (written 609-643 AD). In Qur'an Surah 5:75, we read *"The Messiah, son of Mary, was not but a messenger; [other] messengers have passed on before him."*[10] However, it would be absurd for a prophet of God, who is just human, to claim to be God. Therefore, in order to sustain this view, the Qur'an also denies that Jesus ever claimed to be God; Surah 5:116 says:

"And [beware the Day] when Allah will say, "O Jesus, Son of Mary, did you say to the people, 'Take me and my mother as deities besides Allah?'" He will say, "Exalted are You! It was not for me to say that to which I have no right. If I had said it, You would have known it. You know what is within myself, and I do not know what is within Yourself. Indeed, it is You who is Knower of the unseen."[11]

However, the view that Jesus never claimed to be God is difficult to sustain, given the extensive opposing historical evidence. History is emphatic: Jesus claimed to be God. Believing that Jesus never claimed to be God would have to involve ignoring the evidence. However, to put it directly, if one ignores the evidence, literally anything could be true.

The Lewis Trilemma: Who could Jesus have been?

Once we rule out the possibility of Jesus being a human teacher or prophet, we can conclude that there are three remaining options (as first penned by C. S. Lewis, hence the name):

1. Lunatic: Jesus was just human but was deluded, genuinely thinking that he was God
2. Liar: Jesus was just human and knew it, but tried to convince people he was God
3. Lord: Jesus was telling the truth when he claimed to be God

These three options seem to be the only ones: Jesus either was God or he wasn't, and if he wasn't God, he either knew it or he didn't. We can test these three positions to see which one is backed up by the most evidence.

1. Lunatic Hypothesis

People who claim to be God are not a small group- a quick visit to a hospital psychiatric ward will confirm that. Medics usually label such people as "schizophrenic with delusions of grandeur". Did Jesus exhibit the characteristics of a lunatic?

The view that Jesus was a lunatic is not massively held today, and it was virtually unheard of in the Ancient World. Even enemies of Jesus concluded that he was sane. For example, Josephus, who is one of the most important Jewish Ancient historians, described Jesus as *"a wise man who was called Jesus... And his conduct was good, and [he] was known to be virtuous."*[12], while the Greek satirist, Lucian of Samosata described Jesus as of *"distinguished personage"*[13].

However, I think the most compelling evidence for Jesus' sanity comes from the testimonies of his close followers. If someone persistently claimed to be God, most people would probably eventually ask them to "prove it". It seems logical that people must have asked that of Jesus, and history tells us about two types of proofs people wanted: proof of omniscience by evidence of wisdom, and proof of omnipotence by evidence of miracles.

We read that public intellectuals grilled Jesus on the hi-brow philosophical and theological issues of the time, to test his claims to be God[14]. If Jesus were a lunatic, one can expect that he may have given a lucky, clever-sounding answer once or twice. However, sooner or later, his wisdom would have run out, or at very least, he would have started to contradict himself and make factual inaccuracies. However, it was His disciples, who followed Jesus throughout His entire teaching life, who most vehemently defended the case for Him being God. The people who were in the best position to notice Jesus' insanity came out proclaiming His wisdom.

The other strong piece of evidence that Jesus was not a lunatic is the accounts of His supernatural works. The gospels are packed with reports of Jesus doing supernatural activities: He healed the sick, gave sight to the blind, walked on water, turned water into wine, etc. However, it surprises many to learn that the secular Ancient historians largely agree that Jesus did supernatural deeds. Josephus writes *"About this time there lived Jesus, a wise man, if indeed one ought to call him a man. For he... wrought surprising feats"*[15], while the Babylonian Talmud (a collection of Ancient Jewish Rabbinic writings) states that Jesus *"practiced sorcery"*[16]. The Talmud posits evil as the explanation of Jesus' "miracles", but in doing so, affirms that Jesus did indeed do supernatural acts.

It would be possible to attribute "magic tricks" to the supernatural deeds of Jesus. For example, the American magician duo Penn and Teller perform a stage trick in which water appears to turn into wine. However, it would be absurd to hypothesise that Jesus "unwittingly" did magic tricks. If the miracles were tricks, Jesus would have known that he was not a supernatural being, so we would put him in the second category of "liar".

Therefore, from the evidence of widely attested wisdom and apparent supernatural works, I believe we can conclude that Jesus was almost certainly not a lunatic.

2. Liar Hypothesis

Jesus' clever answers to tough questioning and supernatural deeds are explained away by some with the hypothesis that Jesus was a clever and highly prepared liar, with an extensive knowledge of theology, philosophy and magic tricks. Given the historical evidence described thus far, this position seems potentially plausible.

However, there are two pieces of evidence that greatly undermine this view: prophecies and the resurrection.

The Old Testament (the first 39 books of the Bible, written several hundred years before Jesus) contains more than 300 prophecies about God's promised Messiah. Every single one of these was fulfilled in the life of Jesus. When asked if Jesus could have fulfilled the prophesies by chance, Jewish theologian Louis Lapides replied:

"The odds are so astronomical that they rule that out. Someone did the math and estimated that the probability of just eight prophecies being fulfilled is one chance in one hundred million billion. That number is millions of times greater than the total number of people who've ever walked the planet!"[17]

It is simply a mathematical impossibility that Jesus fulfilled the Old Testament prophecies by chance.

There are some prophesies about Jesus' life that Jesus could have controlled, for example: that He would ride into Jerusalem on a donkey[18], He would teach in parables[19], He would be silent before His accusers[20], and so on. These have led some to postulate that Jesus treated the Old Testament like a script, and simply "acted out" the prophesies.

However, there are many prophesies over which Jesus could have had no control, if he were just a man, such as: He would be born in Bethlehem[21], He would be preceded by a messenger[22], He would be betrayed by a friend[23], He would be crucified with thieves[24], people would gamble for His garments[25], His bones would not be broken[26], He would be buried in a rich man's tomb[27], etc.

The other common explanation is that people edited the Old Testament after Jesus and added in the prophesies. This appeared to be a reasonable and seemingly untouchable argument, up until the discovery of the Dead Sea Scrolls in 1947. The discovery was of a cave about eight miles south of Jericho, containing large jars in which leather scrolls of Old Testament books had been preserved in excellent condition. These scrolls dated to around 100 BC[28]. The discovery was ground-breaking; it showed that the prophesies really had been written before Jesus' lifetime. As renowned theologian Roger Carswell put it: *"Jesus is the only man in history whose biography was written before He was born!"*[29]

All these facts point towards Jesus being more than just a clever, well-prepared man. His claims to be God, wise teaching, supernatural deeds and fulfilment of prophesies seem to leave only one logical option; He was indeed God!

However, there is one final piece of evidence that, in my view, seals the case for Jesus being God- the events surrounding Jesus' death and apparent resurrection. This is what our final chapter will be all about.

5. Historical Evidence Part 2

The Resurrection:
The Minimal Facts Argument

The death and resurrection of Jesus is the single piece of evidence on which the apostle Paul staked his entire faith and ministry. In 1 Corinthians 15:14, Paul writes to the 1st Century church in Corinth (central Greece):

"And if Christ has not been raised [from the dead], our preaching is useless and so is your faith." [1]

This is a huge claim, as the resurrection is an alleged historical event that can be tested from many angles.

Was Jesus really crucified?

The crucifixion of Jesus is a historical fact that is virtually unanimously accepted by historians. As one would expect, all four gospels recount the crucifixion of Jesus. However, this one fact is also corroborated by a huge number of extra-biblical documents from a spectrum of authors.

Josephus, the Jewish historian writes:

"About this time there was a wise man who was called Jesus... When Pilate, upon hearing him accused by men of the highest standing among us, had condemned him to be crucified, those who had in the first place come to love him did not give up their affection for him."[2]

Tacitus, the Roman writes:

"Christus [Greek word for Christ]... suffered the extreme penalty during the reign of Tiberius at the hands of our procurators, Pontius Pilatus"[3]

In the Babylonian Talmud we read:

"On the eve of Passover they hanged Yeshua the Nazarene. And an announcer went out, in front of him, for forty days [saying]: 'He is going to be stoned, because he practiced sorcery and enticed and led Israel astray. Anyone who knows anything in his favour, let him come and plead in his behalf.' But, not having found anything in his favour, they hanged him on the eve of Passover"[4]

The name "Yeshua" translates through Greek to the English as "Jesus", and the word "hanged" was a way of referring to crucifixion.

It is almost unheard of for a single event in Ancient History to be corroborated by so many different trusted writers. The crucifixion of Jesus is therefore a historical fact that is accepted by almost every scholar of the field.

Did Jesus' followers believe they had seen Him risen?

This is a second fact about the death of Jesus that is virtually universally accepted by historians. Upon Jesus' arrest and crucifixion, one can hardly imagine how His disciples were feeling. Their close friend had been taken away to be executed, they feared they were next and nowhere in Jewish Messianic tradition did it allow for God's promised Messiah to die. Therefore, Jesus' death would have demolished the hope and faith of the disciples, who had spent three years believing and preaching that Jesus was the Messiah promised in the Old Testament.

This makes the change of behaviour and attitude of the disciples post-crucifixion, truly spectacular. Three days after Jesus' crucifixion, the disciples were proclaiming they had seen Jesus alive and history tells us that they were all prepared to suffer and die for preaching this one fact. This led to almost all of their martyrdoms; the list is harrowing[5]:

- **Matthew** - killed by stabbing as ordered by King Hircanus, c. AD 60-70
- **James, son of Alphaeous** – crucified, AD 45
- **James, brother of Jesus** - thrown down from a height, stoned and then beaten to death at the hands of Ananias, c. AD 66
- **John** - tortured by boiling oil, exiled to Patmos, AD 95
- **Mark** - burned during Roman emperor Trajan's reign
- **Peter** - crucified upside-down by the gardens of Nero on the Vatican hill, c. AD 64
- **Andrew** - crucified on an "X" shaped cross by Aegeas, governor of the Edessenes, c. AD 80
- **Philip** - stoned and crucified in Hierapolis, Phrygia, AD 54
- **Simon** - crucified in Egypt under Trajan's reign
- **Thomas** - death by spear thrust in Calamina, India, AD 70
- **Thaddaeous** - killed by arrows
- **James, son of Zebedee** - killed by sword by order of King Herod Agrippa I of Judea, AD 44
- **Bartholomew** - beaten, flayed alive, crucified upside down, then beheaded, AD 70

Even the leading German critic of the resurrection, Gert L‚demann, admits *"It may be taken as historically certain that Peter and the disciples had experiences after Jesus' death in which Jesus appeared to them as the risen Christ."*[6] We can thus be in no doubt that the disciples were totally convinced that they had seen the risen Jesus.

In addition, we also have the testimonies from the early church which indicate that many Christians believed that they had seen Jesus alive after his death. In 1 Corinthians 15:3-8, Paul writes:

"For what I received I passed on to you as of first importance: that Christ died for our sins according to the Scriptures, that he was buried, that he was raised on the third day according to the Scriptures, and that he appeared to Cephas [Peter], and then to the Twelve. After that, he appeared to more than five hundred of the brothers and sisters at the same time, most of whom are still living, though some have fallen asleep. Then he appeared to James, then to all the apostles, and last of all he appeared to me also, as to one abnormally born."[7]

This little passage is very significant for a couple of reasons.

The book of 1 Corinthians was written by Paul between 55 and 57 AD. In chapter 15:3-8, Paul is quoting a creed that had been formulated by the early church and given to him, probably during his first meeting with the apostles in Jerusalem in 35 AD[8]. In order to have the creed formulated by the time it reached Paul, it would have originated in church teaching considerably before 35 AD. Given that Jesus was most probably crucified in 33 AD, it is likely that the creed was formulated within a few months of Jesus' crucifixion. This is unprecedented in Ancient World history. Alexander the Great's earliest biographies were written by Arrian and Plutarch, over 400 years after Alexander's death in 323 BC, and yet most historians accept these as reliable. Very few events of Ancient History were documented within 100 years of the event, and (with the exception of the New Testament) there are almost none that fall within a decade, never mind within *months*. Therefore, the documentation of Jesus' crucifixion, resurrection and post-mortem appearances are at the highest level of historical reliability.

Paul also claims that Jesus appeared to over 500 people at once, post-crucifixion. This is a huge assertion and one which some have postulated to be a lie. Imagine if 500 witnesses testified to a crime in court; the jury would have the surest verdict in history! However, Paul (perhaps expecting scepticism) immediately follows with *"most of whom are still living, though some have fallen asleep."* This is Paul effectively saying "some of the witnesses are alive, so go check for yourselves!"

All of these point emphatically towards many 1st Century Christians testifying to the fact that they had seen the physically risen Jesus.

Did sceptics believe that they had seen the risen Jesus?

Not only do we have the testimonies of the early Christians, but we also have accounts of people who were totally opposed to Jesus, but who subsequently became (literally) diehard Christians upon claiming to have seen the risen Jesus.

One obvious testimony to mention is Saul of Tarsus, who later became the apostle Paul (the same man who wrote 1 Corinthians). Saul was, by any definition, an enemy of Christianity. He was a Pharisee who actively persecuted Christians by destroying churches, raiding Christians' homes, and imprisoning Christians[9]. He also witnessed and approved of the stoning of the apostle Stephen for preaching the gospel[10]. However, something happened that turned this enemy of Christianity, into the most influential Christian preacher in history (bar Jesus), who was willing to be arrested and martyred for his faith in Jesus[11]. The explanation of his radical transformation has already been mentioned in 1 Corinthians 15- he claimed that the risen Jesus appeared to him.

Another testimony that is worth mentioning is that of James, the brother of Jesus. From the gospel accounts, we read that Jesus' siblings did not believe he was the Messiah. John writes in his gospel *"even his [Jesus'] own brothers did not believe in him"*[12] while Mark recounts *"Then Jesus entered a house, and again a crowd gathered, so that he and his disciples were not even able to eat. When his family heard about his, they went to take charge of him, for they said, 'He is out of his mind.'"*[13] However, a life-changing event caused James' attitude to dramatically shift, leading him to become a church leader, and eventually the head of the Church in Jerusalem[14]. And as previously mentioned, he was willing to be beaten to death for his faith in his brother Jesus.

The transformations of hardened sceptics indicate that they experienced something extraordinary and unmistakeable; they claimed to have had a personal meeting with the resurrected Jesus.

This is a third fact that historians almost unanimously agree on: some of Jesus' sceptics genuinely believed that they had seen the risen Jesus.

The Minimal Facts Argument

Prof. Gary Habermas is the world's leading scholar on the historical crucifixion and resurrection of Jesus. In his book *The Case for the Resurrection of Jesus*, Habermas and his co-author Prof. Michael Licona established that these three facts (the crucifixion of Jesus, the testimonies of Jesus' followers to have seen the risen Jesus, and the testimonies of sceptics to have seen the risen Jesus) are accepted as true by almost all scholars of the subject. They consequently penned the *Minimal Facts Argument*, which simply takes these three uncontested facts and attempts to draw the most logical conclusion. What is the best explanation of these three facts?

There are many theories that try to explain away the resurrection. Below are the most popular theories (in approximate order of popularity):

1. Body Theft Theory
2. Hallucination Theory
3. Substitution Theory
4. Swoon Theory
5. Evil Twin Theory
6. Super Alien Theory

Theory 1: Did the disciples steal the body?

This is the commonest theory to explain away the resurrection, and one that first appeared within days of the crucifixion of Jesus[15]. We can test this theory against the 3 uncontested facts, to see if it fits the evidence.

1. Does Body Theft Theory fit with the crucifixion of Jesus?

    Yes. Jesus was crucified, so it is possible that the disciples stole the dead body.

2. Does Body Theft Theory fit with the testimonies of Jesus followers?

    No. If Jesus' disciples stole the body, they would have known that Jesus had not risen from the dead. It is therefore unthinkable that the disciples were willing to suffer and die for a claim (Jesus had risen) that they knew to be a lie. People die for causes that they think are true; no-one dies for a cause that they know is false. Or in other words, liars make bad martyrs.

3. Does Body Theft Theory fit with the testimonies of sceptics?

    No. Even if the disciples had stolen the body to make the tomb appear empty, they could not have made Jesus' living body appear to sceptics.

Theory 2: Were the post-mortem appearances just hallucinations?

It is a known medical phenomenon that people whose loved-ones die can sometimes hallucinate appearances of the deceased.

1. Does Hallucination Theory fit with the crucifixion?

    Yes.

2. Does Hallucination Theory fit with the testimonies of Jesus' followers?

   No. Hallucinations are rare and when they occur, they are only ever experienced by one person. (The leading theories of hallucinations involve neurotransmitter imbalances in the brain of the individual[16].) The idea that Jesus' post-mortem appearances were hallucinated by all eleven faithful disciples is a medical impossibility, notwithstanding the 500 people that Paul wrote about in 1 Corinthians. As former legal journalist and editor Dr. Lee Strobel puts it: *"500 people hallucinating Jesus' [post-mortem] appearance would have been a bigger miracle than the resurrection!"*[17]

3. Does Hallucination Theory fit with the testimonies of sceptics?

   No. Hallucinations of the deceased are experienced by those who wish the person were still alive. However, it is pretty implausible that the sceptics and enemies of Jesus would have also hallucinated Him.

Theory 3: Was Jesus replaced with someone else?

This is an interesting theory that is held by the majority of (but not all) Muslims. It stems from the Qur'an's explicit claim that Jesus did not die on the cross. Surah 4:157 says:

"And they said we have killed the Messiah Jesus son of Mary, the Messenger of God. They did not kill him, nor did they crucify him, though it was made to appear like that to them."[18]

One of the Hadith documents (teachings of Muhammad), follows up by saying:

"Just before Allah raised Jesus to the Heavens, Jesus went to his disciples... He then asked, 'Who among you will volunteer for his

appearance to be transformed into mine, and be killed in my place. Whoever volunteers for that, he will be with me [in Paradise].' One of the youngest ones among them volunteered...and Jesus said, 'You will be that man,' and the resemblance of Jesus was cast over that man while Jesus ascended to Heaven from a hole in the roof of the house. When the Jews came looking for Jesus, they found that young man and crucified him."[19] Most (but not all) Muslims believe that Judas Iscariot was this substitute.

1. Does Substitution Theory fit with the crucifixion?

    Possibly. Although Substitution Theory could be used to explain the historical accounts of Jesus' crucifixion, the theory is based on a view of God who partook in mass deception. This seems to run contradictory to the Islamic view of God as being of highest moral good.

2. Does Substitution Theory fit with the testimonies of Jesus' followers?

    No. The arguments would be the same as Body Theft Theory. If the Hadith passage is correct, the disciples knew that Jesus did not rise from the dead, and therefore would have been martyred for a claim they knew to be false.

3. Does Substitution Theory fit with the testimonies of sceptics?

    No. The Hadith passage describes Jesus' immediate ascension to Heaven, leaving no possible chance to appear to sceptics such as Saul of Tarsus and James.

Theory 4: Could Jesus have survived the crucifixion?

Swoon Theory is the theory that Jesus did not die on the cross; he was severely injured, but recovered in the tomb, and then with the help of his disciples. This is a view held by some atheists and some Muslims.

1. <u>Does Swoon Theory fit with the crucifixion?</u>

    No. Roman crucifixion was a barbaric ordeal, in which the cruellest implements and the most effective execution techniques came together to produce that highest level of pain and highest certainty of death. In the whole of human history, not a single person has been recorded to have survived a full Roman crucifixion[20]. In addition, the Roman executioners would have crucified Jesus in the knowledge that Jesus had been previously claiming that He would die and rise again[21]. Therefore, the idea that they mistakenly let him survive is decidedly doubtful.

    On top of this, in 1986, William Edwards, Wesley Gabel and Floyd Hosmer published an article in the Journal of the American Medical Association investigating the medical evidence for the death of Jesus. Their unequivocal abstract read:

    *"Jesus of Nazareth underwent Jewish and Roman trials, was flogged and was sentenced to death by crucifixion...Modern medical interpretation of the historical evidence indicates that **Jesus was dead** when taken down from the cross"*[22]

2. <u>Does Swoon Theory fit with the testimonies of Jesus' followers?</u>

    No. Even if Jesus had survived a full Roman crucifixion, he would have come to the disciples very close to death and in need of intensive medical care. Therefore, the idea that the disciples mistook these battered remains of a man for the gloriously risen Messiah of God is pretty far-fetched.

3. <u>Does Swoon Theory fit with the testimonies of sceptics?</u>

    Highly unlikely. The transformations in the lives of Paul and James indicate spectacular and unmistakable encounters with the risen Jesus. I do not think that a man who had just about survived a full Roman crucifixion would have been capable of synthesising such spectacular encounters.

Theories 5 and 6: Evil Twin and Super Alien Theories

Once the first four theories have been answered, subsequent theories start getting quite desperate and into the realm of science-fiction. The ideas that Jesus had an evil identical twin who came into any documented evidence three days after the crucifixion, and that Jesus was a metamorphosing alien, are genuine theories I have had posed to me! I won't go into the arguments for and against these theories here, but as you can probably imagine, they collapse very quickly under scrutiny.

Theory 7: The Resurrection

Once the above 6 theories have been exhausted, there is (in my view) only one remaining possible option: that Jesus really died, and then was really brought back to life.

1. <u>Does Resurrection Theory fit with the crucifixion?</u>

    Yes. The resurrection requires Jesus to have definitely died. The crucifixion provides this certainty.

2. <u>Does Resurrection Theory fit with the testimonies of Jesus' followers?</u>

    Yes. If Jesus rose and appeared to all of His followers for long enough for them to verify it was Him, this would explain their confident proclamations of Jesus' resurrection.

3. <u>Does Resurrection Theory fit with the testimonies of sceptics?</u>

    Yes. As with the followers, Jesus' resurrection would have allowed Him to appear to sceptics in a way that enabled them to verify it was indeed Him.

Conclusion of the Historical Evidence

At the end of this, the lengthiest chapter of this short booklet, it is worth summarising with one of the most common questions I am asked: "Why do you choose *faith* over *evidence*?" I firmly hold to the view that Christian faith is not "belief in spite of the lack of evidence", as accused by many atheists. Rather, I believe that Christian faith is: *trust in someone securely based on the evidence.*

In my view, the historical evidence points emphatically towards Jesus claiming to be God, dying on the cross, and then authenticating His claim by fulfilling prophesies and rising from the dead.

Therefore, the Christian faith can be summarised as:

- trust that God exists, based upon the evidence that He has revealed Himself to us in the man of Jesus[23]
- trust that God loves us, based upon the evidence that when He was on Earth, Jesus died for us[24]
- trust that Jesus can rescue us from our inexorable deaths based upon the evidence that c.2000 years ago, He rescued Himself from His own[25].

When I was a sceptic, I believed that an invisible, inaudible, unmeasurable, indescribable God was empirically unverifiable. And to an extent, I was right. God's character, by definition, is largely outside our realm of human comprehension. However, my deductions had missed a crucial fact: God's existence *could* be empirically verifiable *if* He chose to reveal Himself to us in a way that we could understand. This is the fundamental claim of Christianity; c.2000 years ago, God revealed Himself to humanity in the most comprehensible way possible- as another human being. This was the evidence I had been searching for!

Conclusion

I am commonly asked by sceptics of theism: "Why doesn't God make Himself more obvious?" I think that through the universe, humanity and Jesus, God has made Himself very clear. However, it does stand to reason that He could make Himself clearer. Perhaps God could write "made by God" on every atom, or speak audibly to everyone on the planet. However, God's desire is not to simply prove His existence to us per se. He also wants to enter a personal relationship with us[1].

Jesus did not come to Earth to simply proclaim the existence of God; He came with a bigger message. Jesus explained that all human beings are sinful, and the punishment for sin is death and eternal separation from God[2]. This place of eternal separation from God is what the bible calls "Hell".

However, in 1 Peter 2:24, Peter writes *"He [Jesus] himself bore our sins in his body on the cross, so that we might die to sins and live for righteousness; by his wounds you have been healed."*[3] On the cross of crucifixion, Jesus took our sin upon himself, and with it, the punishment of death that *we* rightly deserve. By going to the cross, Jesus granted us the gift of forgiveness[4], so that we may be reconciled with God and live with Him in paradise for eternity[5].

So what are we to do with this message? John 1:12 says *"to all who did receive Him [Jesus], He gave the right to become children of God"*[6]. The gift of forgiveness is free and available to all who accept Jesus. And Jesus taught that we accept Him by *repenting*[7]- which means turning away from our sinful way of living, and asking Jesus to be our Saviour, Friend and King. So here is one final question to end this little booklet: could you accept Jesus into your life?

Recommended Reading

Want to dig a little deeper into the topics discussed in this booklet? Here are a few titles that I and others have found helpful.

General Christian Apologetics

- *Richard Bewes,* Top 100 Questions
- *Roger Carswell,* Grill a Christian
- *William Lane Craig*, On Guard- Defending Your Faith with Reason and Precision
- *Timothy Keller*, The Reason for God

Science

- *John Lennox,* God's Undertaker- Has Science Buried God?
- *John Lennox,* God and Stephen Hawking- Whose Design is it Anyway?
- *Lee Strobel,* The Case for a Creator

Philosophy

- *William Lane Craig*, Reasonable Faith- Christian Truth and Apologetics
- *John Lennox*, Gunning for God- Why the New Atheists are Missing the Target
- *C. S. Lewis,* Mere Christianity
- *Alistair McGrath,* Why God Won't Go Away- Engaging with the New Atheism

History

- *John Dickson,* The Christ Files- How Historians Know What They Know About Jesus
- *Amy Orr-Ewing,* Why Trust the Bible?
- *Josh McDowell,* Evidence that Demands a Verdict
- *Lee Strobel,* The Case for Christ

Testimonies

- *Dot Carswell*, Real Lives
- *C. S. Lewis,* Surprised By Joy
- *Nabeel Qureshi*, Seeking Allah Finding Jesus

Notes

Chapter 1: The Existence of the Universe
1. *"Cosmological Argument for the Existence of God"*, Macmillan Encyclopaedia of Philosophy (1967), Vol. 2, 232 *ff*.
2. Summary of argument by William Lane Craig, *On Guard* (David C Cook, 2010), 75
3. Stephen Hawkings, *The Beginning of Time* Lecture (1996)
4. Arvind Borde, Alan Guth and Alexander Vilenkin, *Inflationary spacetimes are not past-complete,* arXiv: gr-qc/0110012v2 (14th January 2003)
5. Alexander Vilenkin, *Many Worlds in One* (New York: Hill and Wang, 2006), 176
6. Summary of argument by William Lane Craig, *On Guard*, 99
7. Stephen Hawking and Leonard Mlodinow, *The Grand Design* (Bantam, 2011), 180
8. John Lennox, *Gunning for God: Why the New Atheists are Missing the Target* (Lion Hudson plc. 2011), 31-32
9. As argued by William Lane Craig in, *"God and Cosmology"* debate with Sean Carroll (Greer Heard Forum, 2014)
10. Anthony Aguirre and John Kehayias, *"Quantum Instability of the Emergent Universe,"* arXiv; 1306.3232v2 [hep-th] (19th November 2013)
11. As summarised by William Lane Craig, *On Guard*, 77
12. Adolf Grünbaum, *The Pseudo-Problem of Creation in Physical Cosmology, in* John Leslie (ed.) *Physical Cosmology and Philosophy* (New York: Macmillan Co., 1990)
13. Immanuel Kant, *Critique of Pure Reason* (New York: Macmillan Press., 1965)

Chapter 2: The Fine-Tuning of the Universe
1. William Lane Craig, *On Guard*, 109
2. Summary of argument by William Lane Craig, *On Guard*, 113-118
3. In case you are interested, the sternocleidomastoid is a muscle in the side of the neck which contributes to the tipping and rotating of the head.
4. John D. Barrow and Frank J. Tipler, *The Anthropic Cosmological Principle* (Oxford University Press, 1986)
5. Richard Dawkins, *The God Delusion* (Transworld Publishers, 2006), 187-188 (emphasis added)
6. Summary of critique by William Lane Craig, *On Guard,* 120-122

Chapter 3: The Morality of Humanity
1. Richard Dawkins, *River out of Eden* (Basic Books, 1995), 133
2. David Hume, *A Treatise of Human Nature* (Oxford: Clarendon Press, 1739)
3. C. S. Lewis, *Mere Christianity* (William Collins, 2012), 16-18 (emphasis added)
4. Summary of argument by Ravi Zacharias, *Nonsense or New Life*, rzim.org/a-slice-of-infinity (9th May 2012)
5. For more of my thoughts on the creation/evolution debate, visit: www.benjaminchangblog.com/creation-vs-evolution
6. Definitions from *Standford Encyclopaedia of Philosophy*
7. 2 Timothy 2:2

8. 2 Timothy 3:16
9. Romans 2:15
10. Job 28:24
11. Psalm 147:5
12. Romans 5:8 (NIV)
13. John 1:1-18

Chapter 4: The Historical Jesus
1. Nabeel Qureshi, *Untitled Lecture at Georgia Tech University* (4th November 2013)
2. Richard Dawkins, *The God Delusion*, 122
3. *Lennox vs. Dawkins- Has Science Buried God?*, hosted by Fixedpoint Foundations (2009)
4. John 10:30 (NIV)
5. John 8:58-59 (NIV)
6. Gary Habermas, *The Verdict of History* (Monarch Books, 1990), 169
7. Pliny the Younger, *Letters* 10.96 (emphasis added)
8. Lucian, *The Death of Peregrine,* 11-13 (emphasis added)
9. C. S. Lewis, *Mere Christianity,* 54-56
10. Qur'an Surah 5:75 (Sahih International)
11. Qur'an Surah 5:116 (Sahih International)
12. Josephus, *Antiquities, XVIII,* 33
13. Lucian, *The Death of Peregrine,* 11-13
14. Eg. Mark 2:18-22, Mark 10:1-12, Mark 12:13-17, Mark 12,18-27
15. Josephus, *Antiquities* 18.63-64
16. *The Babylonian Talmud*, transl. by I. Epstein, vol. III, Sanhedrin 43a, 281
17. Lee Strobel, *interview in The Case for Christ* (Zondervan, 1998), 246
18. Zechariah 9:9 and Matthew 21:1-11
19. Psalm 78:2 and e.g. Matthew 13:1-52
20. Isaiah 53:7 and Mark 15:16-20
21. Micah 5:2 and Matthew 2:1
22. Isaiah 40:3 and Matthew 3:1-12
23. Psalm 41:9 and Matthew 26:14-16
24. Isaiah 53:12 and Luke 23:32
25. Psalm 22:18 and John 19:24
26. Psalm 34:20 and John 19:31-34
27. Isaiah 53:9 and John 19: 38-42
28. Amy Orr-Ewing, *Why Trust the Bible?* (IVP, 2008), 46
29. Roger Carswell, *Real Lives Mission Week, All Souls Church* (2014)

Chapter 5: The Resurrection
1. 1 Corinthians 15:14 (NIV)
2. Josephus, *The Antiquities of the Jews,* 18.63-64
3. Tacitus, *Annals*, 15.44

4. *The Babylonian Talmud,* Sanhedrin 43a
5. List compiled by Josh McDowell, *Holman Bible Dictionary,* op. cit. pp. 118-122
6. Gerd L.demann, *What Really Happened to Jesus?*, trans. John Bowden (Louisville, Kent.: Westminster John Knox Press, 1995), 80.
7. 1 Corinthians 15:3-8 (NIV)
8. Craig Blomberg interview with Lee Strobel, *The Case for Christ,* 44
9. Acts 8:1-3
10. Acts 7:54-8:1
11. E.g. Philippians 1:21
12. John 7:5 (NIV)
13. Mark 3:20-21 (NIV)
14. Hegesippus, *5th book of Commentaries*
15. Matthew 28:11-15
16. Key papers:
a. M. Laruelle, A. Abi-Dargham, C.H. van Dyck, et al. (1996). *"Single photon emission computerized tomography imaging of amphetamine-induced dopamine release in drug-free schizophrenic subjects".* Proc. Natl. Acad. Sci. U.S.A. 93(17): 9235–40.
b. H.M. Jones, L.S. Pilowsky (2002). *"Dopamine and antipsychotic drug action revisited".* British Journal of Psychiatry 181: 271–275
17. Lee Strobel, *Is it Reasonable to Believe Jesus Rose? Lecture,* at Thrive Conference (2013)
18. Qur'an Surah 4:157 (Sahih International)
19. Al-Nasa'I, *Al-Kubra,* 6:489
20. As argued by Nabeel Qureshi, *Did Jesus Really Rise From the Dead?*, event at Emory University (10th April, 2014)
21. Matthew 12:38-40
22. William D. Edwards, Wesley J. Gabel, Floyd E. Hosmer (1986). *On the Physical Death of Jesus,* JAMA. 255(11) (emphasis added)
23. Hebrews 1:1-3
24. Romans 5:8
25. 2 Corinthians 4:13-14

Conclusion
1. E.g. Revelation 3:20
2. Romans 3:23, Matthew 13:40-43, John 3:5-8
3. 1 Peter 2:24 (NIV)
4. Romans 3:26
5. E.g. John 3:16
6. John 1:12 (NIV)
7. Luke 5:31-32, Luke 24:46-47